Poetry for Students, Volume 15

Staff

Editor: Anne Marie Hacht.

Contributing Editors: Michael L. LaBlanc, Ira Mark Milne, Pam Revitzer, Jennifer Smith, Daniel Toronto, Carol Ullmann.

Managing Editor, Content: Gary Braun.

Managing Editor, Product: David Galens.

Publisher, Literature Product: Mark Scott.

Literature Content Capture: Joyce Nakamura, *Managing Editor*. Madeline S. Harris, *Associate Editor*.

Research: Victoria B. Cariappa, *Research Manager*. Sarah Genik, Tamara Nott, Tracie A. Richardson, *Research Associates*. Nicodemus Ford, *Research Assistant*.

Permissions: Maria L. Franklin, *Permissions*

Manager. Shalice Shah-Caldwell, Debra Freitas, *Permissions Associates*.

Manufacturing: Mary Beth Trimper, *Manager, Composition and Electronic Prepress*. Evi Seoud, *Assistant Manager, Composition Purchasing and Electronic Prepress*. Stacy Melson, *Buyer*.

Imaging and Multimedia Content Team: Barbara J. Yarrow, *Manager*. Randy Bassett, *Imaging Supervisor*. Robyn V. Young, *Project Manager*. Robert Duncan, *Senior Imaging Specialist*. Dan Newell, Luke Rademacher, *Imaging Specialists*. Leitha Etheridge-Sims, Mary Grimes, David G. Oblender, *Image Catalogers*. Lezlie Light, *Imaging Coordinator*. Christine O'Bryan, *Graphic Specialist*. Dean Dauphinais, *Senior Image Editor*. Kelly A. Quin, *Image Editor*.

Product Design Team: Pamela A. E. Galbreath, *Senior Art Director*. Michael Logusz, *Graphic Artist*.

Copyright Notice

Since this page cannot legibly accommodate all copyright notices, the acknowledgments constitute an extension of the copyright notice.

While every effort has been made to secure permission to reprint material and to ensure the reliability of the information presented in this publication, Gale neither guarantees the accuracy of the data contained herein nor assumes any responsibility for errors, omissions, or discrepancies. Gale accepts no payment for listing;

and inclusion in the publication of any organization, agency, institution, publication, service, or individual does not imply endorsement of the editors or publisher. Errors brought to the attention of the publisher and verified to the satisfaction of the publisher will be corrected in future editions.

This publication is a creative work fully protected by all applicable copyright laws, as well as by misappropriation, trade secret, unfair competition, and other applicable laws. The authors and editors of this work have added value to the underlying factual material herein through one or more of the following: unique and original selection, coordination, expression, arrangement, and classification of the information.

All rights to this publication will be vigorously defended.

Copyright © 2002
The Gale Group
27500 Drake Road
Farmington Hills, MI 48331–3535

All rights reserved including the right of reproduction in whole or in part in any form.

ISBN 0-7876-5254-7
ISSN 1094-7019

Printed in the United States of America.
10 9 8 7 6 5 4 3 2 1

Porphyria's Lover

Robert Browning 1836

Introduction

"Porphyria's Lover," which first appeared as "Porphyria" in the *Monthly Repository* in January 1836, is the earliest and most shocking of Robert Browning's dramatic monologues. The speaker—or, perhaps more accurately, thinker—of the poem recounts how he killed his illicit lover, Porphyria, by strangling her with her own hair. He does so to keep her his forever, reliving his story to justify his actions and preserve the moment of her death. The simple language and precisely structured form of the sixty-line poem combined with its asymmetrical rhyming pattern suggest a complex madness concealed beneath the speaker's outwardly calm manner and reasonable tone.

The poem's themes of sex, violence, and madness were of particular interest to Victorian readers, who reveled in sensational tales of horror and depravity despite societal condemnation of all things immoral, but Browning overturns normal expectations of such stories by presenting the sex between Porphyria and her lover as natural, making the reader consider the relationship between sex and violence, and exploring the complex nature of the speaker's madness. The result is a study of human nature and morality that poses more questions than it provides answers. The reader is left wondering, for example, whether to believe the mad narrator's account, how to understand society's condemnation of sexual transgressions, and why sexuality is so often linked with dominance and power. The widely anthologized poem is also considered one of the finest poetic explorations of criminal pathology, an early example of Browning's treatment of the theme of experiencing an infinite moment, an ironic reaction against the Romantic idealization of love, and a work that shows a skilled use of lyricism to present the complex workings of a character's mind.

Author Biography

Browning was born in 1812 in Camberwell, a suburb of London. His father, a bank clerk, had a 6000-volume book collection, from which Browning read widely. Most of Browning's education came at home from his artistically inclined, nonconformist parents. It is believed he was proficient at reading and writing by age five and by age fourteen had learned Latin, Greek, and French. At ten, Browning attended Peckam School, where he remained for four years. In 1825, he received a volume of Percy Shelley's poetry and was utterly taken with it, declaring himself a devotee of the poet. In 1828, Browning enrolled at the University of London but soon left, preferring to read and learn at his own pace.

In 1833, Browning's first work, the long poem "Pauline," was published anonymously. The dramatic poem "Paracelsus" appeared in 1835 to lukewarm reviews. "Porphyria's Lover" was published a year later in a small monthly magazine and received scant attention. During the next few years, Browning wrote several unsuccessful plays and a difficult, obscure long poem, "Sordello." From 1841 to 1846, he published a series of poems under the title *Bells and Pomegranates*, which were poorly received at the time but that include some of his best-known poems. *Bells and Pomegranates* includes the poems "Pippa Passes" and "My Last Duchess."*Dramatic Lyrics*, in which "Porphyria's

Lover" appeared untitled with "Johannes Agricola" under the general title "Madhouse Cells," was published in 1842, and *Dramatic Romances and Lyrics* appeared in 1845. Again, while Browning received no critical recognition for these works, later commentators note that the techniques developed through the dramatic monologues during this period—including his use of conversational verse, rhythm, and symbol—are Browning's most important contribution to poetry, influencing such major twentieth-century poets as Ezra Pound, T. S. Eliot, and Robert Frost.

While Browning failed to garner popular and critical recognition for his poetry, it won the admiration of the renowned poet Elizabeth Barrett. The couple met in 1845 and in 1846 eloped to Italy, where they lived together until her death. Barrett demonstrated her love for her husband in *Sonnets from the Portuguese*, and he dedicated his collection of poems *Men and Women*(1855) to her. The volume, which includes the famous monologues "Fra Lippo Lippi" and "Andrea del Sarto," is now regarded as one of Browning's best works, but it received little attention when it appeared; at the time, Browning was known chiefly as Barrett's husband.

After Barrett's death in 1861, Browning returned to England. The appearance in 1864 of the collection *Dramatis Personae* finally brought Browning critical and popular acclaim. In 1868–1869, he published *The Ring and the Book*. The enormously popular work established Browning's reputation, and thereafter he was considered one of England's greatest living poets. His 1880 prose narrative *Dramatic Idylls* brought him international fame. In the last years of his life, Browning received various honors, including a degree from Oxford and an audience with Queen Victoria. He died in 1889 in Venice on the day that his final volume of verse, *Asolando*, was published. Browning is buried in Westminster Abbey.

Poem Summary

Overview

The action of "Porphyria's Lover" unfolds through the recounting of the events of one night—culminating in the murder of Porphyria—by the speaker of the poem. Because the story is not retold to an audience but seems rather to be replayed in the mind of Porphyria's lover, it is somewhat inaccurate to refer to him as the poem's "speaker," but most commentators refer to him as such. Browning masterfully builds up tension in the poem by gradually revealing to the reader, through details provided by the speaker, what has taken place. As it also becomes clear that the narrator is mad, it is up to the reader to decide to what extent to believe the speaker's statements. The poem is a dramatic monologue told by Porphyria's lover (who is never named in the poem), and like other Browning monologues, what is learned about this person is to be gained not merely from what he says about himself but from what he does not say and from a sense that his depiction of himself may not be completely trustworthy. The speaker describes how his lover comes to him one night and he kills her, and in doing so he preserves their love forever. And while his portrayal of the situation is designed to show that his actions are justified, it becomes apparent that he is not so certain of this. In this poem Browning offers a complex psychological study of an insane man who uses reason and argument to explain and make sense of his actions.

Lines 1–5

The poem opens by setting the scene—it is raining, and a storm is raging outside—and with it establishes the tone of the action that follows. The storm is described in simple, direct language: it sets in early, it tears down tree limbs, and its force disturbs the calmness of the lake. The storm is also personified in a way that anticipates the mood of the speaker. Browning here uses a device called "pathetic fallacy," in which something nonhuman is endowed with human intentions and feelings. The wind, the speaker explains, is "sullen"; it destroys the trees out of "spite," and it deliberately tries to "vex," or anger, the lake. Later in the poem the speaker is sullen and he uses his sullenness to elicit some type of reaction from Porphyria. Also in these first few lines, it is learned that the events described are from the recent past; the speaker refers to "tonight." The mood of the speaker is made clear when he explains that he listens to the storm raging outside "with heart fit to break"—he is suffering greatly over something, and the weather outside mirrors and intensifies his feelings.

Media Adaptations

- The Victorian Web maintains a Browning web page at http://landow.stg.brown.edu/victorian/rb/ with links to other interesting sites.

- The audio collection entitled *Robert Browning: Selected Poems*(1984), edited by William C. DeVane, contains a representative selection of dramatic monologues, dramatic romances and lyrics, and short poems that are annotated and are supplemented by an introduction, a list of principal dates in Browning's life, and a bibliography.

- *Robert and Elizabeth Browning* (1998), a video in the Master Poets Collection, presents an overview of the lives, careers, and relationship of these two prominent Victorian poets.

Lines 6–15

Porphyria enters the speaker's cottage, and immediately the tone of the poem changes. In line 4, the speaker introduces himself as passively listening to what was going on outside, but in his description of Porphyria, he presents a woman who busily and actively moves around. In these ten lines in which Porphyria is depicted, Browning uses an abundance of verbs, which show her as performing no less than twelve actions. However, even as she "shut," "kneeled," "made," "rose," "laid," "untied," etc., there is no sense that she is in a hurry or frenzy. Rather, she is in control of her brusque, purposeful movements, which are emphasized by the use of monosyllables. Porphyria enters the cottage and "straight," or right away, gets to work. Her presence shuts out the cold and storm, again an indication of her strength of personality. Despite the fact that there is a storm raging outside, there is no fire burning, and she sets about making one "blaze up." From this the reader gets a sense of her forcefulness but also of the speaker's passive and depressed state, as he has apparently been sitting alone in his cottage in the middle of a storm without attempting to warm the place up.

Indeed, throughout the poem, there are clear contrasts between Porphyria and her lover. She is described in terms of bright color (her yellow hair, the fire she makes blaze up, her blue eyes and rosy face), while he is pale. She is active, he is passive; she is talkative, and he is silent; she come in after being with many other people, while he sits alone and isolated in his cottage. After she makes the fire, Porphyria rises and takes off her clothes that are wet and soiled from the storm. The poet makes clear that it is only after she has put the scene in order that she approaches her lover. It is learned that Porphyria unties her hat, lets her hair down, "And, last, sat down by my side." The use of commas around "last" further emphasize that she goes to her lover only after she has set her surroundings right. She then calls to him.

At least one critic has argued that the portrayal of Porphyria in these early lines of the poem suggests that she is a vampire, or at least that the speaker presents her as one to justify his later murder of her. The setting of the poem, this critic suggests, is typical of the traditional Gothic horror story, as a mysterious lady enters at night during a storm. Porphyria "glides" into the cottage in the silent manner of the undead, and she shows her forcefulness and dominance in her actions before trying to seduce her victim. The rest of the poem, it is contended, provides further evidence of the speaker's belief in Porphyria as vampire, as he thinks her gaze weakens him and his only choice is to kill her, and as he believes that God has not punished him because in killing the vampire he has saved his soul. The name "Porphyria," too, it is claimed, has links with anti-Christian elements: "porphyre" designates a type of serpent, Porphyrius was an anti-Christian philosopher, and "porphyry" is a type of marble that is sensitive to light in the same way that vampires are said to be.

Lines 15–30

The speaker does not respond to Porphyria's call after she sits next to him. This failure to respond indicates his sullenness; perhaps he is even in a catatonic state. Interestingly, the speaker does not even present himself as "I," and the sense of his passivity is stressed once more when he says that "no voice replied" to her calls. Porphyria again is the active partner, as she puts her arm around the speaker's waist and bares her shoulder to him. She proceeds to seduce him, moving her blonde hair from her shoulder, pressing his cheek against it, and then enfolding him in her long tresses. By modern standards, this description may not be considered sexually explicit, but in early Victorian poetry this would be considered a daring and erotically charged scene. The fact that the woman dominates and controls the situation is, of course, unusual, and this aspect is made all the more shocking when it is learned in the next few lines that she is a married woman of a different social class than the speaker. These facts are not immediately obvious, and the reader only gleans from several hints offered by the speaker that the two of them are engaged in an illicit love affair. He explains that Porphyria murmurs to him how much she loves him. But, he says, she is too weak, despite wanting to very much, to overcome her pride and follow her desire to be his forever. She cannot "dissever," or break, her "vainer" ties. However, sometimes her passion overcomes her and she cannot help but come to her lover. Tonight, for example, she has left a "gay feast" to be with him. Thoughts of her pale, lonely lover cannot keep her at the party, and she has come through wind and rain to be with him. The fact that she was at a "gay feast" indicates that she is from the wealthy classes, and so she has a much higher social position than he, who lives in a cottage. Their love affair would thus be frowned upon because of their different social backgrounds.

The picture of Porphyria in these lines of the poem comes as a contrast to the description of her given earlier in the poem. In lines 6 through 15, the speaker presented a figure of a strong, forceful, dominant woman. Now, he presents her as being weak and unable to do what she actually wants—which is to leave her "vainer ties" and be with him. It is not entirely clear whether in lines 22 to 25 the speaker is merely giving his own explanation of her actions or whether he is offering a mocking reproduction of Porphyria's own narration of her feelings and actions that evening. It is clear that while the earlier portrayal of Porphyria is offered in objective terms, the speaker now presents how he sees his lover in light of his self-importance, frustration, and bitterness. Before, the description was of outward events (the storm, Porphyria's entrance and action), and now the speaker turns inward to present a subjective interpretation of her state of mind and motives. While before she was dominant and in control, coming to him only after she has done what she needed to do, in his mind, she is weak and struggling, torn between the party's allure and coming through wind and rain to be with him.

Lines 31–42

Suddenly the demeanor of the speaker changes, and it seems that all is well and he is happy. But it becomes clear again that what he describes is not presented objectively but from the recesses of his troubled mind. While in the first half of the poem the speaker is depressed and morose, it becomes clear in this part that he is in fact quite mad. It becomes especially difficult to determine what to believe about the account he offers. He says that he looks up at Porphyria's eyes and they are happy and proud. He "knows" at that instant that Porphyria worships him. He is surprised and made proud by this realization, and his feelings intensify as he decides what he should do. In lines 31 to 36, the speaker suddenly uses a series of first-person pronouns: "I looked," "I knew," "my heart," "I debated," "mine, mine," and "I found." He thinks that at "that moment" Porphyria is completely and utterly his, and not only that but she is "fair / Perfectly pure and good." It suddenly occurs to him what he should do, and that thing he finds to do is to take her hair in one "long yellow string" and wind it three times around her throat, strangling her.

There is no description at all of Porphyria's struggle or horror, and according to the speaker, she feels no pain. He insists upon this twice. The reader knows the events cannot have occurred exactly as the speaker presents them, that he gives the interpretation of those events shaped by his demented mind. The speaker imagines that his lover who has trouble leaving her social circle to be with him in fact "worships" him, that she is completely his, and that at the moment she is with him she is perfectly pure. He is taken with the perfection of the moment, and he realizes that what he must do is preserve it. Killing her is the only way he can possess her completely. This act, he suggests, is not to be condemned, since, he insists, his victim feels no pain.

Lines 43–55

After strangling and killing her, the speaker opens Porphyria's eyelids, using a strange simile that is at once grotesque and oddly innocent: he lifts her dead lids as perhaps a child would who opens a flower that holds a bee. Again, her eyes indicate that she is happy: they are laughing and "without a stain"—an unusual occurrence indeed, since Porphyria is dead. The speaker then proceeds to loosen the hair from around Porphyria's neck and kiss her on the cheek, which blushes beneath his caress. Now he props her up and puts her head on his shoulder; he points out that this is the same position they were in before, but now the roles are reversed, and he bears her on his shoulder. The balance of power, it seems, has shifted, after Porphyria has "given" herself to him completely and he has made sure that this will be the case for all time. The speaker explains that as he utters these lines, Porphyria's head is still on his shoulder, smiling and happy and free of its worries and in the state in which it has always wanted to be. He imagines that Porphyria shares in his joy of having stopped the passage of time in the exact moment in which her love for him is complete. She is finally free of all she scorned—perhaps her life in a monied society—and has gained her true love. This strange and disturbing depiction of what is happening is made all the more eerie by the fact that the speaker says that it is Porphyria's head, drooped on his shoulder like a flower, that has these thoughts and feelings.

Lines 56–60

The last five lines of the poem show the speaker sitting still with his dead lover's head upon his shoulder, as he reflects that Porphyria would never have guessed how her darling one wish—to be with her lover forever—would finally be granted. The moment of their perfect love has been captured and preserved for all time. They have sat together in the same position all night, not stirring at all, and this, it seems, is the beginning of an eternity together. Again the speaker tries to convince himself (or the reader) that what he has done is not to be condemned, for he says that even God has not spoken about his act. But he leaves it open that he is himself not absolutely sure of God's approval, as he says that "yet God has not said a word"— indicating that He might still do so. Once again, this seems to imply that the speaker, by presenting or reliving his account of the night's events, tries in his demented state to justify to himself, presenting the situation in such a way as to show how he is not to blame but seeming to feel undercurrents of distress and guilt at his crime.

Themes

Madness

Browning's study of madness in "Porphyria's Lover" is subtly presented. At the beginning of the poem there is little sense that the person who narrates these events is insane. The form of the poem is regular, with a tight *ababb* rhyme pattern. Most of the poem is written in an uncomplicated iambic pentameter, in which every other syllable is stressed, creating a rhythmically soothing beat. The diction of the poem is straightforward (most of the words used are monosyllables), as is much of the description of events presented by the speaker. The poem begins with a simple description of a storm and then moves into a similarly straightforward description of Porphyria's movements. The narrator explains everything methodically, presenting a catalog of his lover's movements, as she shuts out the cold, kneels down, makes a fire, takes off her coat, and sits by his side. However, as is soon made clear, the apparent objectivity of the account and the outward, metrical impression of reasonableness and calmness belie the psychological upheaval in the speaker's mind. As the events of the evening unfold through the speaker's monologue, the reader realizes the speaker is not completely in touch with reality. The sudden shift in the speaker's perception of Porphyria—she is at first a strong, commanding presence and in the next moment is shown as weak and indecisive—indicates that actual events and his interpretation of them are not in accord.

In the second half of the poem, Browning offers more and more clues to show that the speaker is not merely delusional or confused because of his near-broken heart but that he is quite mad. Yet all this is presented, again, in a manner of eerie calm, even as the speaker describes how he takes his lover's hair and twists it around her neck until she is dead. At the moment of her death, there is no shift in rhythm (although the language of the poem does become progressively more metaphorical throughout the poem), and the detachment with which her death is reported makes the scene all the more shocking. At the end of the poem, it is obvious that the speaker has completely lost touch with reality, but again neither the tone nor the diction points overtly to his madness. Rather, the reader gets a sense of his dementia from what the speaker does not say, from how his depiction of events cannot possibly accord with reality, and from the incongruity of his insistence of his lover's happiness with the fact that she lies dead in his arms. Although nowhere in the poem does the poet Browning offer his own commentary on the events that take place or the state of the speaker's mind, with his presentation of Porphyria's lover's account of what takes place, he forces the reader to ask questions about the nature of the speaker's mind and madness. By not writing using disjointed language or crazy rhyme (the rhyme scheme is rather irregular but follows a very orderly pattern), Browning suggests that madness is a complex phenomenon that has more in common with sanity than most people would perhaps like to think.

Sex and Violence

"Porphyria's Lover" is not an overtly sexual poem by today's standards, but its frank depiction of an illicit love affair between a woman of high social standing and her poor lover would have been shocking to Victorian readers. However, Browning's poem is not shocking merely because it presents a transgressive sexual union but because of the way it depicts it. Nineteenth-century readers in England, despite strict societal standards of morality, were fascinated by stories of prostitution, unwed mothers, and torrid affairs, and the newspapers were full of stories catering to the public taste for scandal. Browning does not just offer the shocking story of an illicit affair but complicates it by showing the intimacy and complexity of the relationship and by provoking additional emotional reactions in readers when it is learned that the speaker kills his lover. Browning uses sex and violence in the poem to pose questions to readers about the nature of immorality. In the poem, Porphyria tries to seduce her lover by laying bare her shoulder and putting his head on her shoulder, and he in turn kills her and places her head on his. Both sex and violence were deemed "immoral" by Victorian standards, and Browning seems to be asking why this is as he shows the two acts mirroring each other. What makes these two very different types of acts "wrong" in the eyes of so many people? Why are sex and violence so intimately connected and of such interest to people that they continue to be fascinated with sensational and scandalous stories despite at the same time being horrified by them?

Dominance and Power

The two characters in the poem are lovers, but there is obviously a great deal of tension between them, and there is a sense of the speaker's unease at Porphyria's power. She is clearly more in charge: she is superior to him socially; she comes to see him and puts his house in order. She is a forceful presence as soon as she walks in the cottage and is able to shut out the storm. The speaker seems to resent her power over him. For, while he portrays her as strong and commanding, he insists that she is weak and needs him more than anything else. When he kills her, he finally reverses their roles so that he is in control; at the end of the poem, she sits with her dead head drooped on his shoulder, when before she had lain his cheek on hers. The fact that the woman is the more powerful partner in the relationship is contrary to the stereotype, and this may be the reason for the speaker's resentment and anger. The fact that he cannot control her—she has a gay social life which she enjoys—is a likely source of his bitterness, and the only way to rid himself of his feelings of impotence and powerlessness are to kill her. Again, while Browning offers no commentary on the nature of power in relationships, the poem brings up questions about how power dynamics manifest themselves in sexual partners' attitudes and behavior toward each other.

Topics for Further Study

- Compare and contrast "Porphyria's Lover" with another of Browning's dramatic monologues, such as "Johannes Agricola" or "My Last Duchess." What similar patterns do you see in the writing? What differs in their tone and style?

- In "Porphyria's Lover," what clues suggest that the speaker's account is unreliable, that what he says cannot be true? What would make you not trust his recounting of what happened?

- Do some research into the

psychology behind crimes of passions. Based on your research, are crimes of passion only committed by those who are mentally unstable, or are "normal" people also capable of such acts?

- Do some research into the way modern U.S. courts evaluate sexually-motivated crimes. Explain how a modern court would address the crime and criminal that this poem presents. What do you consider would be a just punishment for Porphyria's lover? Explain your answer.

- Assume the identity of the speaker and write the defense you would use at your trial to explain the events that led up to the murder.

- Do you think there is evidence in the poem to suggest that Porphyria is a vampire? If so, what is it? If not, why do you think this is not a reasonable interpretation of the poem?

- Research the treatment of the criminally insane in England in the 1860s and their treatment in the United States in 2002. Write a compare and contrast essay that describes how the speaker in this poem would be treated in these different times and places.

Experiencing an Infinite Moment

Time plays an important role in "Porphyria's Lover," which is made up of sixty lines divided into twelve parts using the same rhyme scheme. The use of sixty lines (reflecting the minutes in an hour) made up of twelve clock-like sets might be Browning's way of emphasizing the significance of temporality. From the beginning, when he tells us the rain set in early tonight, the speaker is aware of time. When he describes Porphyria's weakness at not being able to leave her other life behind to be with him, he insists that she wants to be with him "forever." The speaker, in his delusional state, believes that by killing Porphyria he can preserve forever "that moment" of their perfect love, and he feels his action is justified because he has captured for all time the beauty of their relationship. His replaying of the scene in his mind—and thus the poem itself—seems also to be an attempt to stop time and experience forever the moment of their perfect love. This theme of experiencing an infinite moment (in which the lover experiences a woman's perfect love) was common in much Romantic literature, and it has been suggested by a number of critics that in his poem, Browning parodies this notion by showing a madman capturing this infinite moment with his gruesome murder of his loved one.

Style

Dramatic Monologue

"Porphyria's Lover" is a dramatic monologue, a poem in which a speaker talks to a silent listener about a dramatic event or experience. Browning is considered to be one of the earliest and greatest practitioners of this form, and "Porphyria's Lover" is his first poem in this style. The dramatic monologue offers readers intimate insight into the speaker's changing thoughts and feelings because he presents in his own words how he sees and understands the situation he discusses. However, as becomes clear in "Porphyria's Lover," much of what the reader learns about the speaker of the monologue comes not from the speaker's own revelations but from what he does not say. The speaker in "Porphyria's Lover," for example, never declares that he is mad, but the reader infers from his words that he must be. The speaker also means to convince (perhaps himself) that his actions are justified, but there are clues that he may not actually feel this way, and certainly the reader can decide, after considering what has happened, how the speaker should be judged. One of the most interesting features of the dramatic monologue is that it presents a situation through the words and thoughts of a particular character, but then it is up to the reader to decide to what extent that character's actual depiction of the events should be believed.

With "Porphyria's Lover," the reader must determine by reading between the lines of the speaker's account how reliable a narrator he is, how accurate his portrayal of Porphyria is, what his intention is in recounting the story, and exactly what is the extent and nature of his madness.

Form

"Porphyria's Lover" uses a highly patterned structure: it is composed of sixty lines of verse divided into twelve sets of five lines each which rhyme *ababb*. The regularity of the pattern is contrasted with the unusual asymmetry of the *ababb* rhyme, and together they every effectively emphasize the inward turmoil of the speaker's mind. The use of iambic pentameter throughout most of the poem lends it a steady, rhythmic quality, which again contrasts sharply with the unusually disturbing events depicted in the work. Browning uses the highly structured form of the poem to reinforce the speaker's sense of his own calmness and sanity, as he speaks reasonably and straightforwardly about his despicable acts, indicating perhaps that madness is a complex phenomenon that is not always immediately identified as such.

Language

Browning often uses complex classical reference and colloquialisms in his poems, but the content and language in "Porphyria's Lover" seem straightforward and easy to understand. Again, the directness and apparent transparency of what is said by the speaker seem unusual considering that he is a madman whose thoughts should be difficult to analyze. Browning seems to take pains to make the musings of a criminal psychopath clearly understandable to every reader. The poem uses simple, short words. However, there are subtle developments in the poem to suggest the speaker's unusual state of mind and his heightening sense of conflict. At first, the poem relies almost exclusively on straightforward description as the speaker recounts the events that have taken place, but as it becomes clear that the events described are seen through the lens of the speaker's madness, the language becomes more metaphorical. In the early description of Porphyria, the speaker offers a simple physical description of her. She has smooth shoulders and yellow hair. But after he kills her, he uses vegetative imagery to describe her—her eyelid is like a shut bud that holds a bee, her head droops like a fallen flower, and it is smiling and "rosy"—which seems to accentuate her total subjection by him. Browning also uses language in other effective ways in the poem. For example, the sense of Porphyria's dominance over her lover and the difference in their temperaments is indicated by the active verbs which initially describe her and contrast her with the speaker's passivity. When the balance of power shifts as he kills her, the speaker reveals himself as in control, and this shift is accomplished by his associating himself with action while she lies passively and silent against him.

Historical Context

Sex and Scandal in the Victorian Era

Strictly speaking, the Age of Victoria should correspond with the beginning and end of Queen Victoria's reign (1837 to 1901), but literary historians generally agree that the Victorian period began around 1830, when many social, political, and economic changes were taking place in English society. The Catholic emancipation of 1829, which enabled Catholics to sit in Parliament; the construction of the first railway in 1830; Parliamentary reform in 1832, extending the enfranchise to the middle classes (now one in five adult males could vote); the suppression of slavery in the colonies in 1833; and the beginning of the world's first industrial revolution meant profound changes in the existing social order. However, despite many positive social reforms, Victorian England was known also for its repressive attitude toward sexuality. This might have been partly as a backlash to the notorious debauchery of the Regency period during the early part of the century. Sexuality in the Victorian period was seen as taboo, not an appropriate subject of discussion. But, paradoxically, while moral purity was the norm in public, sex during the Victorian era was a powerful force in journalism, art, and literature. Sexual scandals were the subject of numerous newspaper stories, and the reading public had a voracious appetite for tales of illicit affairs. "Porphyria's Lover," written by Browning around 1834, during the early days of the Victorian period, takes on a scandalous subject that would have been of interest to the reading public that enjoyed shocking and horrific tales of sexual transgression. However, in his poem, Browning does not merely feed his readers' need for scandal by describing a sordid crime enhanced by madness and violence, but shocks his audience even further and thus forces them to question their desire for sensational stories that both titillate and horrify them.

The repression of sexuality in Victorian England, then, had the effect of unleashing a great deal of discourse about sex. The number of newspapers in Britain also multiplied during this time, and they became cheaper and more widely available. This burgeoning medium generated stories for popular consumption on a scale that had not been possible before. The papers' greater availability, coupled with increasing literacy, made scandals publicly accessible in new ways. It can be argued that the proliferation of sensational sex scandals in contemporary media has its roots in the Victorian era. The point here is that the social and material conditions were met during this period in Western history to make mass consumption of sensational material the phenomenon it continues to be today. Unfortunately for women, the double standards used to judge their sexual behavior in everyday life also found their way into the scandal sheets, and women suffered far more greatly than men if they were even rumored to be misbehaving sexually. A woman would lose her good name, be barred from society, and decried as "fallen," and because she was usually so completely under the power of her husband, any transgression on her part could mean being outcast for the rest of her life. Another reason that "Porphyria's Lover" is interesting in the context of Victorian social life is that the poem presents a situation in which a woman dominates an illicit relationship and the immorality of that relationship is then undercut by the horror of the murder that ensues. In the poem, Browning once again overturns his audience's expectations by presenting a twist on a scandalous subject that requires them to reconsider their attitudes towards sexuality, propriety, and morality.

Compare & Contrast

- **1830s:** The invention of the steam press, cheaper paper, and increasing literacy in England results in the proliferation of newspapers, including a great number of scandal sheets.

- **Today:** Circulation of tabloids in England such as the *Daily Mirror*, that concentrate on scandalous stories, far exceeds that of other daily publications.

- **1830s:** In England, a man has the

legal right to beat and lock up his wife; a woman who leaves her husband is not allowed even to keep what she earns; a man may divorce his wife but a woman must prove cruelty or desertion if she wants to leave her husband. She is not able to obtain a divorce.

- **Today:** In the United States, statistics show that women experience more than ten times as many incidents of violence (including murder) against them by their spouses or partners than do males.

- **1830s:** In England, middle-and upper-class men were expected to have affairs, but the slightest hint of scandal that a woman had a sexual relationship outside marriage meant social ostracism.

- **Today:** In the United States, more men than women are reported to commit adultery, but more women than men file for divorce to get out of bad marriages.

Critical Overview

"Porphyria's Lover" was published early in Browning's career in the first issue of the journal *The Monthly Repository* under the title "Porphyria." It received little notice upon its initial publication in 1836, and critics were similarly unresponsive when it was reprinted in 1842 in *Dramatic Lyrics* together with a companion piece "Johannes Agricola" under the general title, "Madhouse Cells." When it appeared again in 1863 in *Poetical Works* under its present title, Browning's reputation had grown, and all his earlier poems were more favorably reviewed than when they were first published, but the work was not singled out for praise. In *Browning: The Critical Heritage*, which includes all major critical assessments of Browning's works in his lifetime, "Porphyria's Lover" is mentioned but twice, and at that only briefly and in passing. The English writer Charles Kingsley writing in 1851 is said to have disliked it, but an anonymous 1876 critic refers to it as an example of a good short poem by Browning. In general, in the nineteenth century the poem seems to have been seen as one of a handful of immature verses written by a young Browning during a period when he was writing poetry in the confessional style and developing his techniques of the dramatic monologue.

In the twentieth century, Browning's reputation in English literature having been firmly established, "Porphyria's Lover" was heavily anthologized but presented to be "of interest" by most critics almost solely by virtue of its being a "murder" poem, an example of Browning's interest in criminal psychology and violence, and Browning's first dramatic monologue. However, as the critic Norton B. Crowell points out in his study of Browning's works, the poem "rarely received the attention it deserves." Most of the analyses of the poem were brief and covered single aspects of the poem.

An interesting but largely discredited interpretation of the poem was offered in 1900 by James Fotheringham, who claimed that the lover in the poem is dreaming and the entire action takes place in "wild motions" of his brain. C. R. Tracy's 1937 *Modern Language Notes* article, one of the first devoted entirely to a discussion of the poem, argued that the speaker of the poem is not mad, or at least no more so that others of Browning's characters. Several critics have dismissed the poem as minor and unimportant. Thomas Blackburn writing in *Robert Browning: A Study of his Poetry* in 1967, for example, complained that the work is "unleavened by insight," and Park Honan in *Browning's Characters* regarded it as an "extremely good anecdote" but essentially echoes the sentiments of the earlier critic J. M. Cohen that the work is a "juvenile and unrepresentative horror poem."

Recent commentators have tended to see the poem as more interesting and complex. While they agree that "Porphyria's Lover" certainly does not rank as one of Browning's most sophisticated works, they have pointed out the psychological complexity of the anonymous narrator, seen its indebtedness of earlier works such as John Keats's "Eve of St. Agnes" and William Shakespeare's *Othello*, recognized the use of techniques developed by Browning in his more mature monologues, suggested that the speaker views his lover as a vampire, and noted that the poem is an interesting study in abnormal psychology that anticipates Browning's most influential work.

What Do I Read Next?

- "My Last Duchess," published in 1842, is perhaps the most celebrated of Browning's dramatic monologues. It presents in fifty-six lines the thoughts of the Duke of Ferrara about his late wife, but as much is revealed about the coldness and inhumanity of the duke as about his gracious and exquisite wife.

- Browning's early lyric "Johannes Agricola in Meditation," which was published together with "Porphyria's Lover" in *Dramatic Lyrics* in 1842 under the general heading of "Madhouse Cells," is also a study of madness, in this case of religious mania.
- Margaret Atwood's *Alias Grace*(1996) reconstructs the sensational story of a 16-year-old Canadian housemaid named Grace Marks who was tried for the murder of her employer and his mistress.
- *Dark Dreams: Sexual Violence, Homicide, and the Criminal Mind* (2001), by Roy Hazelwood and Stephen G. Michaud, reveals the twisted motives and thinking that go into sexual crimes.
- *Darkness Visible: A Memoir of Madness* (1992), by William Styron, describes the author's own descent into depression and madness.

Sources

Blackburn, Thomas, *Robert Browning: A Study of his Poetry*, Eyre & Spottiswoode, 1967.

Cohen, J. M., *Robert Browning*, quoted in Park Honan, *Browning's Characters: A Study in Poetic Technique*, Yale University Press, 1961, pp. 28–30.

Crowell, Norton B., *A Reader's Guide to Robert Browning*, University of New Mexico Press, 1972.

Fotheringham, James, *Studies in the Poetry of Robert Browning*, Paul, Trench, 1887.

Honan, Park, *Browning's Characters: A Study in Poetic Technique*, Yale University Press, 1961, pp. 28–30.

Tracy, C. R., "Porphyria's Lover," in *Modern Language Notes*, Vol. 52, No. 8, December, 1937, pp. 579–80.

Further Reading

Curry, S. S., *Browning and the Dramatic Monologue*, Haskell House, 1965.

> Curry claims that Browning invented a new language with the dramatic monologue, which might account for why critics were slow to embrace his work.

Dupras, Joseph, "Dispatching 'Porphyria's Lover,'" in *Conversations: Contemporary Critical Theory and the Teaching of Literature*, edited by Charles Moran and Elizabeth F. Penfield, National Council of Teachers of English, 1990, pp. 179–86.

> Dupras expresses the difficulties he encountered in teaching "Porphyria's Lover" to his students and explains that when a teacher forcefully determines a poem's "meaning" to other readers, the poem dies.

Pearsall, Robert Brainard, *Robert Browning*, Twayne Publishers, Inc., 1974.

> Pearsall provides a straightforward account of Browning's career as a whole and attempts to say something useful or interesting about every book and every poem that Browning published.

Sutton, Max Keith, "Language as Defense in

'Porphyria's Lover,'" in *College English*, Vol. 31, No. 3, December, 1969, pp. 280–89.

> Sutton shows how this poem spoken by a madman extends the reader's awareness of how the mind works and reveals what madness is like by following the speaker's train of thought.

Lightning Source UK Ltd.
Milton Keynes UK
UKHW020622190419
341311UK00013B/709/P